*To Ann
with all good wishes
Michael*

HORIZON

POEMS FROM
THE ISLE *of* MAN

MICHAEL CURTIS

By the same author
Making Tracks .... Platform Poets, 1984
The Shape of Happiness .... Aegis Press, 1994
In Deepest England .... Redbeck Press, 1997
Two Poems by Post with Philip Bennetta .... Community of Poets Press, 1998
Serotonin Days .... Redbeck Press, 2001
Red Meat Dreams .... Redbeck Press, 2003
Presences with Barbara & Russi Dordi .... Picture-Poems, 2005
Long Haul .... Redbeck Press, 2005
Taking Shape – Selected Poems 1984-2005 ...... La Maison de la Poesie, Nord/Pas de Calais, 2006
Weeks .... Urban Fox Press, 2007
In The Affirmative .... Redbeck Press, 2008
Walking Water .... Editions des Vanneaux, Picardy, 2009
Four Poems by Post
   with Philip & Sue Bennetta .... Community of Poets and Artists Press, Charente, 2011

*The Scarpfoot Zone: An Anthology of
Contemporary Poetry from Kent*
Editor with John Rice and David Shields ...... Aegis Press, 1996

For children

The Black Hound .... The Manx Experience, 2006
Melnais suns (The Black Hound and Poems) ... Daugava, Riga, 2010

Acknowledgements
Erin, Flora, Gravity, Gob y Deigan, Lobster, Niarbyl and *Sparrows* were first published in *Under the Hill*, Isle of Man Poetry Society, and *Balladoole* in *Dream Catcher*.
Fauna was first published in *Real Imaginings*, Doghouse Press, County Kerry, and *Laxey* in *The Island Now*, Isle of Man Poetry Society.
Bride was first published as a Mandeville Press Dragoncard.
Gob y Deigan also featured in the 2012 Manx LitFest Poetry Trail.

Versions of several poems were published in previous collections.

Horizon: Poems from The Isle of Man © Michael Curtis 2012.
Illustrations by Julia Ashby-Smyth.

The rights of Michael Curtis to be identified as the author of this work has been asserted in accordance with Sections 77 and 78 of the Copyright, Designs and Patents Act 1988.

All rights reserved. No part of this book may be reproduced, stored in a retrieval system, or transmitted, in any form or by any means, electronic, mechanical, photocopying, recording or otherwise, without the express written permission of the publisher.

ISBN: 978-1-907945-21-2

Published by: Lily Publications Ltd, PO Box 33, Ramsey, Isle of Man IM99 4LP
Telephone +44 (0) 1624 898446.   www.lilypublications.co.uk

CONTENTS

Geometry 5
Weightless 6
Headlong 7
Gravity 8
God's Tears 10
Flora 11
Wild Garlic 12
Fauna 13
Cormorant 14
Harrier 15
Sparrows 16
Home Birds 18
Takeover 19
Gobbag Vooar 20
Element 22
Laxey 23
Lobster 24
Cautions 26
Before 28
Bubbles 29
Sight 30
Annexe 31
Bends 32
Balladoole 34
Wrecked 35
Property 36
Knockaloe 38
Erin 40
Breath 41
Shore Hotel 42
Niarbyl 44
Gob Y Deigan 45
Lhiannag 46
Calf 48
Bride 50
Snaefell 51
Mull 52
Sartfell 53
Returned 54
Forecast 55
Islands 56
Edge 57
Feline 58
Horizon 60
Stormed 62

Geometry

With little to go on
I failed to fathom

the closed geometry
of village life

found no way
through the maze of names

that filled the endpapers
of the family bible

described a circle
fixed on you alone, until

you threw a line to find me
stranded on the curve

and the warm radius of your love
drew me to the centre

where still I study
properties and angles.

Weightless

No Saxon in you, but Celt, Viking
and a thousand years
taking it one day at a time

fishing, farming, keeping low,
ducking the Revenue, passed to king
or favourite, bought and sold

till dead seams forced emigrants
to new worlds, homesick pioneers
now scaled to philately.

When Dumbells collapsed grandpa
went back for Gwello gold
but the dust took his lungs, widowed

young, grandma presided black
over a clutch of coddled sons, slow
to marriage, never to leave home.

You, too late to live in mourning,
took off for the city, met me
always looking for my paradise island

yours in your pocket, nestling
weightless, with little need
of the markers I'd clip to its wings.

Headlong

Late afternoon
we walked up to the cairn
north of the harbour

came to the cliff face
that brinks the grey jags
stark out of the clambering sea

where whales flow unseen
slow sharks bask
and dolphins gather.

Backs flat on strong grass
our feet heeled the precipice
as the headland rose beneath us

then two startled sheep
crackled through the gorse
dashed to a sheer, pathless place

before suddenly turning back
shying from the sharp air
that led them on

and you told me about the dog
went too far, raced over
into headlong space.

Gravity

We walked back down
to the river, harbour, shore
and sat on the warm wall
where a rush of children
fetched up from school.
Jinny divers crossed, gulls
floated on air and water

but one seemed different,
described a wider compass
across the bay, repeatedly
threw sharp white W's
into the bubbling currents,
wings of balsa, longer
fuselage fitted for oceans.

We exchanged binoculars,
speculated what it might be,
never thinking the greedy
gulping name used to tease
childish appetites belonged
to this inexhaustible fisher.
Two, three more joined in

rising in deliberate rings
through easy space, dipping
the horizon, regaining
height, catching gravity to fall
in dead-eyed vision
and scissor the whitened sea
with soundless explosions.

God's Tears

June washes down the mountain
on torrents of western wind.

Spotted orchids ripen in the soil
co-habit with disease, letting
fungus succour them

under a stone wall
hemlocks duck uncertain weather
coax their deadly eight foot high

the sycamore by their side
bides its time, takes a hundred years
to spread its gathered canopy.

In the wide open air
fuchsias feel far too wild
for bee or hawk moth to powder

shower red waterfalls
onto borders and pavements
cascading tropical tears

that lament another end
to sun struck beginnings -
but they'll be happy to try again.

Flora

Flowers forget our names.
Common or Latin slip through
a Spring shower's footfall
but keep their own particulars.
Acrobatic bold throws lateral
red valerian from stone walls,
purple and gold blend high ground
coincidence of gorse and heather,
fern damp valleys stitch yellow
ditch buttons of celandine.
Careless of identity, primrose,
sorrel, wood anemone intermingle,
upper decks of wild garlic
take the air, bluebells stalk
what woodland they can find
to map archives of ancient oak.
Salted squill and thrift brighten
the rhythm of coastal walks,
poppies play at orchids, moss,
liverwort and crusty lichen
act as clean air monitors.
Plants too luxuriant, abundant
and full of themselves
to compare, pin down, glass,
never forget their signatures
or how to spell their names.

Wild Garlic

It was a relative of chives and first sign of spring

eaten by waking bears
        to cleanse themselves and restore their strength.

The island put on lavish displays

brilliant green blades broke the soil of damp meadows
                      in dappled shade, along stream sides.

It repelled moles
a pervasive smell telling it from toxic Lily-of-the-Valley

                      was favoured by fairies
who gathered star-shaped flowers as the leaves lost pungency.

Like the cool ground it grew in
        it was material, held hostage to earth, and invasive

though it died back entirely when its seeds had ripened
                let other plants grace the same place

and if some trace did remain
            it would wait out of sight like something prior

                      an idea
that passed, if imperfectly, between minds.

Fauna

The clucking gulls know I've no designs on them or theirs
describe their necessary circles in the air, suspend
slow creaks of wings, small downbeat wheezes

land for the next relentless stint of nesting
stumbling back to bicker and fidget
in the high nooks behind me.

My eyes are for the sea
unstirred, uninterrupted,
stiller than glass that cannot melt

but puckered by indolent black-backs
free from sentry duty as cormorants cross
and re-cross between their bobbing indifference.

No doubt about identity, no question whether
animal, vegetable, mineral, wave or fin,
feathered or furred head

no scramble to the water's edge
clutching a camera, spumed rock mistaken
for shark or whale, no uncertainty on this defining day.

Elements exchange, worlds sample
and I settle to mine, reminded
of others all around.

Cormorant

crosses the Sound
on a skimmed progress of mist

carries above the rocks
and pungencies of ozone
a precarious sprig of kelp

and disappears in the horizon

leaving hard white waves
to ledge insurmountable cliffs
assist grey seals into sunshine

or trouble the trippers from Port Erin
hurdling heavy currents to the Calf

and me to wait out a wingless sky.

Harrier

A mirror to the sky
flashed you down from the mountain
where rain distracted prey
and cloud had closed the hills
to the oval glitter in my garden

liner tucked under the lawn
flat stones from Cornaa
polished with wind and rain
rocks rinsed clean of soil
to anchor smuggled lilies.

I waited for you to find me
in your unattended descent
to be grasped by your talon
examined, committed to memory
before you rose to fill

falling night, my mind
with wide-wing definition,
unhurried flight, fan tail
inscribing your reflection
on my striped eye.

Sparrows

Unstoppable crows
carve soft western airs
with swoops of black severity

supercilious gulls
commandeer the promenade
to grip railings like prey

sharpened gannets
tack hard as they plunge
into a conflict of currents.

And the sparrows?

They gang up in the hedge
fanning out
to mob new-mown lawns

risk the open greenhouse
pick off the easy ants
summer heat evokes

play hide and seek
with a pushy blackbird
who scoffed the fallen apples
and thinks he owns the place.

Having long ago mastered
the old disappearing trick

they're never there
when that pair of magpies
comes clacking

materialising
three gardens down
chasing their tails.
A racket of togetherness.

Home Birds

When we come back to the house
the sparrows have fledged.
They congregate in an apple tree,
scatter, land, daintily double-hop
a softening of daisies and buttercups
across the one week lawn, quarter
the grass for seeds and grubs, dart
in and out of the holed hedge, skirt
the pond I laid (now it's obvious)
for them, take ownership of slates,
larvae, slowly unscrolling lilies,
strafe the greenhouse, drill a wedge
where glass and metal join, drawn
by young bunched grapes that fall
to heavy verticals, sometimes thud
solid air that shouldn't be there,
retreat to a branch, recalibrate reality
(it doesn't take long) restart
their song, take me out of my skin,
locate me in a wider world
we both can share, their delight
in me entirely in my head, mine
in them wild and free and limitless.

Takeover

Apples will redden, ripen, fall for slowing wasps,
grapes fur and shrivel on the greenhouse floor,
the long-awaited lily will blossom and grace
the pond throughout a warm September, lush grass
will thicken round roses, chickweed steadily stick,
two dozen parson pigs squeeze through plugholes
to retake bath and basin, marshalled ants sally forth
in spells of glassy heat to colonise the oleander,
occasional showers will rinse soot on the fireplace,
tiles will wriggle free from grout, the invisible crack
in the chimney let in a little damp to stain the wall,
that radiator will persist with its unstoppable drip
till we come back in Spring and disturb the peace.

Gobbag Vooar

Twelve metres, seven tonnes, they'll leap
clean out of the water. Head south-west,
May to September, morning or evening.

For each on the surface dozens more beneath.
When a tall dorsal cuts diagonal across the bay
imagine the rest, pulsing shadow, jaws agape,

following food detected off Cork or Cornwall,
zooplankton the current warms. Dangerous?
You're the danger. Nets, propeller blades.

See the scars, the deep V sliced from a fin?
Switch to neutral, keep your distance.
Flash startles. Don't even think about jet skis.

We know so little. Their abiding mystery
leads us past the crowded cafe
to scan the horizon from a headland

where we station our expectant selves,
learning to read water, see through light
and forget time. Be still against the hill

and wait until they join us from a world
we struggle to share, no more or less
than what they always were, oceans breathing.

Can we grasp their element, its deep enormous ease?
Their strength and size, teeth that pose no threat?
When will we be ready for that?

Element

Sown in crevice and nook
a dozen parents and pups
dry under a white sun
beached two tidal metres
above untroubled water
the flat cormorant scans

furred bellies swell
for herring gulls to clean
heads loll to fishless air
then flop down again
backs scratch razor rocks
that rise to their spines.

One prises loose, flips
and wobbles, slow rolls
on bulbous seaweed, tips
from side to side down
the buckled ledge, teeters
over a diving shelf, drops

out of clumsiness, falls
from laborious reality
to a swifter elemental self
after all the trials
of a foreign land, slips
into the teeming sea.

Laxey

Mother and son skim the waves
little sister shrieks *It's cold*,
a white yacht nudges eternity
fern cliffs darken emerald.

I fall for coves and caves
into childhoods lived, relived, still living
track August from the Shore Hotel
and Beach Café to sucked shingle

where Dick nearly drowned that day
or you posed by the harbour wall
in beatnik black, rewinding
the Laxey lives we made our own.

Up the hill, past the echoing school
you still leap the long loop of time
chanting skipping rhymes while Tom
looks on in growing desperation

and at King Orry's Grave all tunnels
to the burial chambers turn
to tell the living from the dead,
but it's easy to ignore the lines.

Lobster

Father and son
try unaccustomed waters
on the Traa Dy Liooar
to haul up pots
two hundred yards from shore

sorted last night
in the usual manner
over a pint at the bar
men among men
mother and child upstairs.

A small blue buoy
fidgets on the line
tugging colours that
fall to invisibility
under the undulating sea

the engine cuts
abrupt silence, he leans over
emptiness, lugs into the light
a hidden den
of scratch scuttling lobster

brilliant red and blue
stalk eye and claw
shine in the glazed sun
for half a minute
before death sets in

pink, unmoving, matt.
After that the boy
has little to say,
silenced by the way unknowns
rise up to be known and die.

Cautions

Before you go
just to make sure
I'll herb your clothes

and spread yellows
round the door,
primrose, marigold.

Let the storm subside
and wait indoors
here by the window

that boat's too old
it's not fit for
such awful weather.

After it grows calm
hug the near shore
stay on the safe side

with an eye on the sky.
Don't be late or
your food will get cold.

Now you do know
the water's wide
and if you can't see harbour

you're too far from home.
You'll catch more
if you keep in, close

to the tide's hold.
Take the deep anchor.
Not like the last time

when you sailed
free with your father.
He never told me why.

Before

Though the skill of skimming's still
two summers away play these pebbles
for a time before you enter,
swimming is already a fearless dive
between breakers and the sea stays open,
but not the farthest corner of the sand,
closest to the rocks, where grandpa
loses his legs to the withdrawing swell
and offers you another sketch of death,
swim where the raft spills shining boys
from its sides into gentler depths,
where tall trees rearing on the cliffs
are just an inkling, before high houses
anchor giddy extensions onto air as
two canoes feather the heat-struck waves,
binoculars scan the bay for whales and
children ride body boards after school,
before the moon slows down enough
to be trodden on, or the setting sun
becomes mortal, before all who fall
or swim or rescue here go before, ignore
the cold, now join the waiting water.

Bubbles

Blowing bubbles at sea level
the nursery welcomes a late arrival
toddling across the enormous green
in red cap, shirt and shorts to join
outstretched arms and happy squeals
making waves as they exhale
each wafted wish to heaven
or thin air, till the final
Monday child bustles in with mum
now the washing's on the line.

In time the bubbles find oblivion,
as bubbles will, and ribbon teams
form to foster social skills,
turn and run, drop and gather batons,
attempt to score their goals,
then each well-drilled civilian
stands still, holds hands to crocodile
march up the green hill
as clouds ascend above them
filled with rainbow dreams.

Sight
to Ewan

You'd an eye for a foal,
the ready ewe, top bull in show
when I stood at your side
those sunny Sulby August days
pretending to see it too.

Last time, I saw you nod
to each and every, cloth-capped,
elbows resting on the rail
as they paraded round the yard,
heavy horse and handler,

eyes upon them from the start
you made a quiet appraisal
of Shire, Clydesdale, Part-bred,
Pure for Plaiting, Best Turned Out
Longest Mane, Best Feather

and chose your winners.
But the final prize, Kindest Eyes,
they must award to you
always sharp enough to show
a keen, unblinkered heart.

Annexe

Churchyards ooze confidence.
Inch-perfect headstones,
polished white, showy gold,
shine marbled permanence

or bide their time,
let wind and rain discover
the codes untroubled masons
chiselled in black granite.

It's a walk in the park. Stroll
past plaques, raised kerb beds,
chippings spilling indigo light,
angels, hearts, hills in the distance.

To the west, through a gate
in the corner, a fenced field,
weeded and mown, cultivates
patience, waits to be planted.

Bends

This morning a terse radio
reports last night's mortality
fifty-three, Ramsey, sidecar team

after false starts, rainfall
the racing touch and go
for all the ferried pilgrims.

Today on the Mountain Road
twelve thousand leathered engines
lean into precarious air

wannabees and never weres
throttling Mad Sunday
while racers tune the grandstand.

Tonight behind a steady smile
too slow to read the menu
too quick to take the call

his eyes lack any line
sheered by years of wind
and the surgery of speed.

Tomorrow despite the pull of gravel
he'll approach a double ton
blur wall and kerb and telegraph pole

tilt at corners
and kiss cambers
through twenty-seven hundred bends.

Balladoole

You weren't what they expected
internees scratching
this lip of land for a different age -
iron, bronze, prehistoric.

Linen, knives, shield, buckle
but no sword.

Placed here to show who's boss?
Blend in with the locals?

Or was it the best spot for miles around
your high bracken vantage point

where white spar marks the stern and bow
that bore you to Valhalla's chaos
despite the depredations of rabbits?

And the girl with no grave goods beneath you -
chattel, sacrificial slave, cold corpse?

Did you board her like clinkered oak
and cloak her against the soaking rain

or did you gatecrash her sacred ground
in the last throes of heroism
then cover up the damage?

Wrecked

The brig Lily out of Liverpool
loaded with fire and rum
bound for the African coast
hit the hurricane
drawn to the Sound
despite her anchor

all seemed well for salvage
till smoke rose from a hatch
and an axe cut the deck
to pour water
sparking powder.
Twenty-nine lost.

Tonight all rescued life
has withdrawn from storms
sleeps on inside
invisible tide and reef
while a solitary foghorn calls
the sea to calm.

Property

The last to sail, *Kitty's Amelia*,
was cornered in the triangle
working the African coast

and heavy with Guinea goods,
Maldives shells, Silesian cotton,
arangoes, red carnelian beads,

knives and painted calico,
when the tide of abolition
caught her broadside.

Crow thought it through.
No Liverpool commissions
to the Americas, no vessels

to master or crew, no margins
for the merchants to argue
or East India to undercut,

but no wrecks, fever, wounds,
capture by French privateers,
forced march to a filthy prison.

He'd trade the Dutchman's cargo,
ship the goods to Kingston
get his head money in England,

then, perhaps, purchase an estate
in a better part of the island,
live the life of a gentleman.

Knockaloe

The peloton of cows crosses the field
on a well-worn diagonal

bunches for the final sprint to the line
that carries them over the headland
into the cheering sea.

When the Lusitania went down
and the Empire caught spy fever
the City of Huts grabbed fields

traded trippers for enemy aliens
grew allotments, orchestras, theatres
workshops, a skittle alley

eleven different schools
to teach the treacherous hun

Viennese fiddlers, cockney waiters
who couldn't speak a word of German
before they came here

the art dealer on a short holiday
that lasted five years

old Jacob who played the streets
of Douglas for five decades
moved to streets of barbed wire

his son in the Rifle Brigade
would visit when he could.

The steers are in clover
camped out in the next field
unconcerned and bountiful

between the rubble of internees
they graze vanished compounds

gain three kilos a day
waiting to be requisitioned
for the slaughterhouse.

Erin

We talk across distance, sea and city,
preoccupied space, your voice echoes
on invisible tiles. This sweep of sand

is a desert traversed in miniature
by a small boy marching in the sun
to the oasis of his father's love.

Dogs abound as beach dogs do, chase
sticks, stones, dreams, each other
in the here and now of their daily paradise

and gulls confer with folded wings,
two ducks observing, stalk the small delta
where the flat stream runs out of land.

We ring off. You carry happiness forward
to the tipped seat in the conference hall
that won't quite contain your afternoon

while the lighthouse, caught in scaffolding,
keeps still for its spring makeover and I
prepare for the long separations of summer.

Breath

They all fetch up here
coastal walkers, highway workers,
refuse collectors, snoozing coppers,
for breakfast and a breath.

We all stopped here then,
nans and grandpas, dads and mums,
sons younger and older,
my wife, my self, my former self,

watched the waves, entered them,
crunched pebbles, bounced them
(once to double figure skims)
with or without, together, apart.

I'm waiting for the Fair to start
my heart's unturned engine
and cough back to spluttered life
these stiff pistons of love.

Shore Hotel

Why not let them wander by, the days,
like glazed tourists too long
on a coach to somewhere?
And let this shaded seaside bar
admit a shake of salt from the quay,
soak up the afternoon's remains
on a loud packet of crisps or
one of its thirstiest beer mats?

Why not let plaster crack, wires
search the yellowed ceiling
for a circuit of power like
banyan roots on a mission?
And let Bill hold forth over there,
socks turned over sailor wellies,
then muster the familiar smile
and sink one more Black Label?

Why not while we're able let
the tv in the corner fall mute,
put off tomorrow what we didn't
put off today and natter out
another easy, half-lit hour
as Art's *Only Have Eyes
For You* strokes the dozing collie
and tickles dust on window sills?

Why not, blown on soft June winds,
only have lazy eyes and ears
and tongue for house-brew
and you my lifelong hostelry?
And let summer come and dream
of timeless days and always
wish for more, right here, where
we know we can wait forever?

Niarbyl

A light that can bend and fly
    knows how to skim surfaces like these. A solitary seal
rises and dips, flashes semaphores south to north, nosing
to Iceland, head brimming salt

triangulates the headlands, points the way
    for sharks to bask
in quick procession across the bay, sixty fins
cutting a dash.

    Now the light
that lives in living things
    is sliced by dorsal and tail
until it abandons the water, scatters, hunts

something to inhabit, rock, bladder wrack,
    feather or fur
raises the wings of cormorants
throws three hills to the west, over Bradda

past Erin
bounces down to the Sound, bundles the sun to Kitterland
    skips to the Calf, startles the cairn
shines white streamlines onto the flights of gulls.

Gob y Deigan

Westerned against the next sea
the sun in its high August
children straddling rock pools

I swam a little from the shore
between the widening hills
out towards the lack of land

to a pebble speck of sunshine
where the steady fur brown head
rose from nowhere to seal my fate.

Already mourning our separation
I trod invisible air and water as
languorously he shadowed

circumnavigated me, observed
and bowed and dipped enormous
unhurried, elemental minutes

and in the silence deep below us
every line was washed away
between native and immigrant.

Lhiannag

Twenty years later
early summer, June
via the old railway
from St Germaine's Halt
a new path, alone this time
less sure of my ground

but found the way
scrambled the muddy slope
down to open shore
with small reason to hope
while two Arctic Terns
circled and strafed

treading lightly not
to disturb the singularity
I looked out to sea, wishing
not expecting, and there he was
waiting it seemed
those two quick decades

dog head turned to me
unsurprised, unhurried
on the cold water, saying
join me. I crossed the rocks
and pebbles, went waist-deep
but not to my neck

after a minute's indulgence
as much as I'd earned
he did his disappearing trick
left me standing
looking west, uncertain
of further returns.

Calf

MacLir's enchanted isle
slipped anchor. The Viking Kitter
saved his name but missed the fight
when his coracle went down.

Hermit monks carved stone, raised
keeills. Still couldn't cling on.

The Lord of Mann's coney warren
was abandoned, food for longtails
that scuttled from the wrecks.

Cattle swam across at slack water
horns tied to a straining stern
till the farms cracked in the gales
and gave the grazing back.

The last lighthouse keeper obeyed
orders and beat a retreat

leaving it to butterfly, beetle
storm petrel, chough and puffin,
reserved and observed
by visiting wardens, summer residents

and a pair huddled to binoculars
who stare across the white lick currents
past the gulls, seals, deterrent rocks
and wonder what it would be like to live there.

Bride

Cut out black on grey flannel cloud
crows ride the wind. Replete cows
recline in kale. Gorse travels golden
down to shingle the sea suckles.

Stone gathers to farmhouse and wall
without ornament, elemental,
paddocks clothe hillocks, dropped
from the pockets of careless glaciers.

At the heel of the northern plain
where ice ran out of breath, abrupt hills
indent the horizon. Patrick stepped here
between legends, a village in his toes.

Snaefell

Headlights dip as falling fog
shrouds Manannin's isle

hooded by lowering cloud
the harrier hesitates

denied sight of sea the gull
beats languid on mountain mist

tempted to the humming road
two sheep warm to tarmac

under the slow-breathing bog
peat compresses its laborious harvest.

Six kingdoms from this peak
on a clear day. Today just two:

green immediate beneath our feet,
and above us, somewhere, blue.

Mull

This will be an island
between others
when the levels rise

stepping stone to the Calf
from a chastened isle
the thaw delivers.

Up here vantage is all
and only the west wind
tests its integrity

keeps stone coffins clean
in the slow sharpening circle
of flint, bronze, radar.

Dispassionate as grass
it bares its teeth
to an excitable sky

certain in its elevation
it will wait out the weather
till the waters retreat

and puzzle the settlers
who sweat to its summit
to scan the new horizon.

Sartfell

Barbed horizontals twist
the tensioned four-spike view
puncture the autumn air
and sever sky from swelling sea.

We peer through, past Barregarrow
and Michael to Irish cliffs that rear
false islands in the mist.

The restaurant is closed
where mums and dads would take
afternoon cakes, Sunday roasts
heavy with local meat, strong tea.

Gone too most of them, into
the boundless blue that swallows
all the rust this wire will be

healing each casual scar
that leaves a mark on the luminous
sea and sky, us
and all befores into its after.

Returned

Low birds occupy
the metre of sky
that grey cloud pins
to the mountain road.

A car catches sun.
Its fast semaphore
descends the straight
to Creg Ny Baa

turns hard right
into the fist of cloud
crumpling the valley,
lights up the route

of a daughter returned
to her place of birth.
She slows at the limit
turns left, right again

past the churchyard
where her parents lie
protected from air
by a metre of earth.

Forecast

First, you must understand
despite our best intentions
the sun won't always shine

for much of the time
the best you'll get is high cloud
dispassionate, self-contained.

Next, you need to realise light,
sunlight in particular, is
a given thing and not here every day.

Though we're far from the equator
our weather tends to circle. But
the rain, falling water, precipitation

rinses all. I do mean all. Air,
leaf, stone, horizon, so when it pauses
to let the sharp sky through

you'll delight in your clarity
as in its particulars, radiant as blue
when the day exceeds prediction.

Islands

lead us on
then cast us off
lure us in again
maroon memory
in the presence
of loss, that sense
of coming back

to the woman, man
we might have been
if we hadn't left
to try our luck
one wide open day
and sailed away
to continents

and if we stay
they'll take us in
keep us safe
till home and dry
why risk
a tall ship, chance
the wrecks?

Edge

But stand on the edge of the land
any edge of any land
on a cracked uneven breakwater
signs warned against
as unsettled sea retreats into itself
emptying everything around you
into a deep resonance
as black-backs beat the wind
that ransacks offshore air
and the glimpsed island to the south
always holding station
in sheer accumulation of rock
continues into filtered light -
stand surrounded
by what could kill you
what could make you, raise
your sights, look
past the tethered buoys
waiting for death, past bobbing gulls
that are what they are
beyond the momentary transports
of a backlit horizon
to what you came here for.

Feline

Halved by morning blues
and lacking stars
still the moon
balances above the aerial
to entertain clouds
skidding to the mainland
on a south-westerly.

When I look away
to mark the waking hills
or sketch the day ahead
it will doze
in a corner of the sky
waiting out the afternoon
indifferent, unnoticed

till the blues darken
to backdrop, cloud fluff
folds and disappears
wind rises, rattles
the hinged flap
in night's back door
and its turn comes round.

HORIZON

Out it pads
as cold clings to roofs
a white cat printing
moonlit lawn, scenting
wild possibilities
to turn the contrast up
and shine again.

Horizon

hauls its blues
over serried roofs, rises
above dish and aerial
crows crashing trees
smokeless chimneys.

Sea level
an endless fence
to keep us in, raise
stakes on travel, surprise
logic, quiz visitors, insist

the sun keep its head
above water, paint
in space, fill the time
between dustbin and gull,
ferry and hill, squeeze

air, push clouds
into the corners, stick
to sky like wallpaper,
high seamless flats
erected for audience,

a dado deep enough
to bask sharks, tall enough
to hook fishermen, a rail
to rope dinghies, a road
for skis, the finish line swimmers

never find, salt light
climbing the ocean's back
to dwarf summits, claim
descending jets, lift hearts,
hold eyes.

Stormed

Baled out by November
under late slanted sun
yellow sheep separate
over the barrelled hill
amble up an afternoon
that eases back the clouds
with a whisper of air
and rolls out the valley
to lift the road west
where the future waits
a restless ferry
fidgeting on the ropes
every day a little more
impatient to be gone.

In the locked marina
masts ring the breeze
as an empty harbour
meets the cooling sea
before it sets to winter
turns isolate
and fixes creeks and rivers
retreating to a time
when, an only child,

I stayed inside the mist
that hid the world outside
and screened first dreams
that showed themselves
in any light I chose.

Now they give way
to the eager gales
that scatter them to stars
circle the scoured hills
denuded now of life
skelter across the bay
on white horse waves
and finally find me
up on the high wall
that tried to fool the tides
still looking to the sky
while black storms
curl around my hopes
and carry me away.

Notes

Balladoole A Viking ship burial excavated on a site that also contains prehistoric flints, Bronze Age burials, Iron Age earthworks and a later keeil or chapel. The ship lies within early Christian lintel graves. The woman had no goods and may have been a sacrificial victim or an earlier burial.

Calf The Calf of Man, Yn Cholloo in Manx, is a small island to the south-west of the Isle of Man circled by precipitous cliffs and separated by the Sound, a turbulent tidal race.

Dumbells In February, 1900, Dumbell's Bank, virtually the Manx National Bank, collapsed with severe consequences for the population.

God's Tears A Manx name for the fuchsia.

Gobbag Vooar Manx for Basking Shark (Big Mouth).

Gob Y Deigan/Lhiannag A secluded bay on the west coast of the island, to the north of Peel.

Jinny Divers A Manx name for cormorants.

Knockaloe Knockaloe Farm was a World War I Internment Camp where 30,000 German and Austrian men were held.

Mull The Mull Circle, Meayll (Bare Hill) in Manx, is a late Neolithic/early Bronze Age peninsula burial place where six pairs of cists channel radiating passages. A World War II radar station was sited nearby.

Niarbyl A cove on the south-west coast, called Yn Arbyl in Manx or The Tail due to its long reef jutting out from the shoreline. From here a massive series of rounded headlands stretch southwards towards the Calf of Man.

King Orry's Grave The largest known megalithic tomb on the island lies in the garden of a cottage in Laxey. King Orry was King Godred of Crovan, who took control of the Isle of Man and most of the islands between it and Norway in 1079. Many monuments were named after him.

Manannan
In Manx mythology, the island is ruled by Manannán mac Lir, a Celtic sea god, who draws his misty cloak around the island to protect it from invaders.

Property The last slaving ship to sail from Liverpool on the triangular voyage to Africa, the Americas and back to Britain was Kitty's Amelia under the command of Manx captain, Hugh Crow. In 1807, while she was on the African coast, legislation was passed abolishing the trade by British vessels.

Traa Dy Liooar A Manx saying - Time enough.